To:
Wendy

Within the words of this book,
I would love to give these gifts
to you.

May they bless your life
in many wonderful ways.

Love
Mary

Other books in this series...

Blue Mountain Arts®

A Friend Lives in Your Heart Forever

A Mother Is Love

I Love You Soooo Much
by Douglas Pagels

Keep Believing in Yourself and Your Special Dreams

Sister, You Have a Special Place in My Heart

The Greatest Gift of All Is... A Daughter like You

The Greatest Gift of All Is... A Son like You

I'd Love to Give These Gifts to You

A keepsake collection of encouraging words and special blessings

Edited by Douglas Pagels

SPS Studios™
Boulder, Colorado

Library of Congress Catalog Card Number: 2001005734
ISBN: 0-88396-615-8

We wish to thank Susan Polis Schutz for permission to reprint the following excerpts and poems that appear in this publication: "Go beyond yourself...," "Love is the source of life," and "Sometimes you think that you need to be perfect...." Copyright © 1976, 1986 by Stephen Schutz and Susan Polis Schutz. All rights reserved.

Certain trademarks are used under license.

Manufactured in Thailand
First Printing: January 2002

✪ This book is printed on recycled paper.

Library of Congress Cataloging-in-Publication Data

I'd love to give these gifts to you : a keepsake collection of encouraging words and special blessings / [edited by Douglas Pagels].
        p. cm.
   ISBN 0-88396-615-8 (hardcover : alk. paper)
   1. Conduct of life—Quotations, maxims, etc.   I. Title: I'd love to give these gifts to you.
II. Douglas Pagels.   III. SPS Studios.
   PN6084.C556 I36 2002
   158.1—dc21

                                                                2001005734
                                                                            CIP

SPS Studios, Inc.
P.O. Box 4549, Boulder, Colorado 80306

The Gift of...

The Gift of Welcoming the Wonder

I walk the world in wonder.

— Oscar Wilde

Not knowing when the dawn will come, I open every door.

— Emily Dickinson

*And all the windows
of my heart
I open to the day.*

— John Greenleaf Whittier

*Each day brings with it the miracle of a new beginning.
Many of the moments ahead will be marvelously disguised
as ordinary days, but each one of us has the chance to
make something extraordinary out of them.*

— Douglas Pagels

The Gift of Setting the Stage for Good Things to Happen

You are given a daily invitation
to fill your heart with all the
smiles it can possibly hold.

— Douglas Pagels

Today is big with blessings.

— Mary Baker Eddy

Every day is a fresh beginning,
Every morn is the world made new.

— Susan Coolidge

You may have a fresh start
any moment you choose.

— Mary Pickford

The Gift of Making
Each Day a Masterpiece

A life well lived is simply a compilation of days well spent.

— Douglas Pagels

The game of life is a game of boomerangs.
Our thoughts, deeds, and words return to us
sooner or later with astounding accuracy.

— Anonymous

Then give to the world the best you know
And the best will come back to you.

— Henry Wadsworth Longfellow

Make each new morning the opening door
to a better day than the one before.

— Anonymous

The Gift of an Angel by Your Side

May you always have an angel by your side • Watching out for you in all the things you do • Reminding you to keep believing in brighter days • Finding ways for your wishes and dreams to come true • Giving you hope that is as certain as the sun • Giving you the strength of serenity as your guide • May you always have love and comfort and courage •

And may you always have an angel by your side • Someone there to catch you if you fall • Encouraging your dreams • Inspiring your happiness • Holding your hand and helping you through it all • In all of our days, our lives are always changing • Tears come along as well as smiles • Along the roads you travel, may the miles be a thousand times more lovely than lonely • May they give you gifts that never, ever end: someone wonderful to love and a dear friend in whom you can confide • May you have rainbows after every storm • May you have hopes to keep you safe and warm •

And may you always have an angel
by your side •

— Douglas Pagels

The Gift of Getting Things Done

I arise in the morning torn between a desire to improve
the world and a desire to enjoy the world. This makes
it hard to plan the day.

— E. White

The great thing about life is that as long as we live,
we have the privilege of growing.

— Joshua Loth Liebman

The great thing in the world
is not so much where you are
but in what direction you are going.

— Oliver Wendell Holmes

Your life is a work in progress. That's "progress" —
as in always moving forward, always reaching,
always striving, always making things better.

— Douglas Pagels

The Gift of Good Advice

It is a funny thing about life. If you refuse to accept
anything but the best, you very often get it.

— W. Somerset Maugham

Enjoy when you can, and
endure when you must.

— Johann Wolfgang von Goethe

I avoid looking forward or backward,
and try to keep looking upward.

— Charlotte Brontë

There are times when life isn't all you want,
but it's all you have. So what I say is: Have it!
Stick a geranium in your hat and be happy!

— Anonymous

The Gift of Gentle Words
in Difficult Times

The mantra to help you make it through:
"Need to, can do. Have to, will do."

— Douglas Pagels

If you can walk, you can dance.
If you can talk, you can sing.

— Zimbabwe Proverb

Count your blessings, not your troubles.
You'll make it through whatever comes along.
Within you are so many answers.
Understand, have courage, be strong.

— Douglas Pagels

The Gift of Letting Your Creativity Shine

Be creative! You're the artist here. You're the one who can brush away the clouds and make the sun shine. Paint your own picture, choose your own colors. And forget all that business about having to stay between the lines.

— Douglas Pagels

Every artist dips his brush in his soul, and paints his own nature into his pictures.

— Henry Ward Beecher

To affect the quality of the day — that is the highest of the arts.

— Henry David Thoreau

The Gift of Enjoying It All

Talk with the year which is coming as with a friend who is crossing your threshold to bring you gifts. Say, I welcome you. Let me come close to you; let me walk beside you and listen to all the secrets which you keep in your great soul for my sharing....

If I breathe in your pure airs, if I live according to those natural laws which govern you, if I accept the spring, the summer, the autumn, and the winter of life as perfect expressions... then I, too, may grow.

— Ella Wheeler Wilcox

There is no season such delight can bring
as summer, autumn, winter and the spring.

— William Browne

The Gift of Getting to "Happily-Ever-After"

Each new day is a blank page in the diary of your life. The pen is in your hand, waiting for you to write the very best book you can. Have pages on understanding and tales of overcoming hardships. Fill your story with romance, adventure, learning, and laughter. Make each chapter reflect time well spent. Meet your obligations, but take time to greet your aspirations. If you live up to your potential, you'll never have to live down any disappointment. Remember: Goodness will be rewarded. Smiles will pay you back. Have fun. Find strength. Be truthful. Have faith. Don't focus on the things you lack.

Realize that people are the treasures in life, and happiness is the real wealth. Have a story about doing your best each day, and... the rest will take care of itself.

— Douglas Pagels

The Gift of Keeping Smiles Up and Stress Levels Down

Life is really simple, but we insist on making it complicated.

— Confucius

You don't have to be the one responsible for making everything work. Believe me. The big things are already taken care of: the sun will rise in the morning, the stars will come out at night, and — if you work it right — a child, someone you love, or a dear, close friend will share a special smile with you — and make everything wrong — right again.

— Douglas Pagels

There are only two things in the world to worry over: the things you can control, and the things you can't control. Fix the first, forget the second.

— Anonymous

The Gift of Asking, Believing, Receiving

I ask not for a lighter burden, but for broader shoulders.

— Jewish Proverb

Do not pray for easier lives. Pray to be stronger men. Do not pray for tasks equal to your powers. Pray for powers equal to your tasks! Then the doing of your work shall be no miracle, but you shall be the miracle.

— Phillips Brooks

I ask not for a larger garden, but for finer seeds.

— Russell Herma Cornwell

Keep on sowing your seed, for you never know which will grow — perhaps it all will.

— Ecclesiastes 11:6

The Gift of Believing in Miracles

I swear to you there are divine things
more beautiful than words can tell.

— Walt Whitman

All change is a miracle to contemplate; but it
is a miracle which is taking place every instant.

— Henry David Thoreau

The invariable mark of wisdom is to
see the miraculous in the common.

— Ralph Waldo Emerson

The sun, with all those planets revolving around it and
dependent on it, can still ripen a bunch of grapes as if
it had nothing else in the universe to do.

— Galileo Galilei

The Gift of Rising Up
to Meet Your Potential

If we can put a man on the moon, you can see your way through to where you want to be. There is a way. There is always a way.

— Douglas Pagels

Have the daring to accept yourself as a bundle of possibilities, and undertake the game of making the most of your best.

— Harry Emerson Fosdick

No one knows what he can do until he tries.

— Publilius Syrus

If we did all the things we are capable of doing, we would literally astound ourselves.

— Thomas A. Edison

The Gift of Realizing Your Dreams

Follow your hopes and dreams while you can. While the desire
is burning. When the chance comes your way. Don't be a ship
that stays in the harbor, never straying from its safety. Don't
get tangled up with "maybe... maybe someday." Too many folks
will tell you that if you spend your whole life waiting, "someday"
arrives too little, too late.

Maybe it's already a little later than it seems. If you really
want to do it, do it while you can.
                Be brave... and sail away on your dreams.

— Douglas Pagels

For the people who are always going to do things: The road to
Success lies along the path of Decision, and up the hill of Endeavor,
and across the bridge of Patience. The road to Defeat lies through
the valley of Pretty Soon and the winding paths of Wait-a-While.

— Ella Wheeler Wilcox

There's no traffic jam on the extra mile.

— Anonymous

The Gift of Keeping Worries Away

It is foolish to worry about anything
so temporary as today.

— Anonymous

Worry is like a rocking chair —
it will give you something to do,
but it won't get you anywhere.

— Anonymous

Nothing wastes more energy than worrying.
The longer one carries a problem, the heavier
it gets. Don't take things too seriously. Live
a life of serenity, not a life of regrets.

— Douglas Pagels

The words "peace" and "tranquillity" are worth
a thousand pieces of gold.

— Chinese Proverb

The Gift of Appreciating Life to the Fullest

I may be uncertain about exactly where I'm headed, but I am very clear regarding this: I'm glad I've got a ticket to go on this magnificent journey.

— Douglas Pagels

That it will never come again
Is what makes life so sweet.

— Emily Dickinson

Stoop and touch the earth, and receive its influence; touch the flower, and feel its life; face the wind, and have its meaning; let the sunlight fall on the open hand as if you could hold it. Something may be grasped from them all, invisible yet strong. It is the sense of a wider existence — wider and higher.

— Richard Jefferies

The Gift of Using Time Wisely

One of the secrets of happiness is to take time to accomplish what you have to do, then to make time to achieve what you want to do. Remember that life is short. Its golden moments need hopes and memories and dreams. When it seems like those things are lost in the shuffle, you owe it to yourself to find them again. The days are too precious to let them slip away. If you're working too hard, make sure it's because it's a sacrifice for a time when you're going to pay yourself back with something more important than money could ever be. If you're losing the battle, do what it takes to win the war over who is in control of your destiny. Find time, make time, take time... to do something rewarding and deeply personal and completely worthwhile. Time is your fortune, and you can spend it to bring more joy to yourself and to others your whole life through.

Time is your treasure. And instead of working so hard for it, do what it takes to make it work... for you.

— Douglas Pagels

The Gift of Moving Beyond Your Misfortunes

In the midst of misfortunes, it is well to remember that every mountain must have its valley, every oasis its desert, every rainbow its storm, and every day its night.

— Anonymous

If a door slams shut, it means that God is pointing to an open door further on down.

— Anna Delaney Peale

Misfortunes cannot always be avoided.
But they can be made easier — just by knowing that they will be overcome.

— Seneca

The world is advancing. Advance with it.

— Guiseppe Mazzini

The Gift of Spreading Smiles Around

The sun, as we journey toward it, casts
the shadow of our burden behind us.

— Samuel Smiles

A smile is a curved line that sets things straight.

— Anonymous

Life is a mirror.
If you frown at it,
   it frowns back;
if you smile,
   it returns the greeting.

— W. M. Thackeray

A smile is the light in the window of your face
which tells people that your heart is at home.

— Anonymous

The Gift of Making Today Your Moment in Time

Don't make the mistake of letting
yesterday use up too much of today.

— Anonymous

Leave tomorrow until tomorrow.

— German Proverb

Whether you're eighteen or eighty, I encourage you to
have the courage to find the magic in this day. Go out
of your way to appreciate the deserving things here before
you: people who matter, places that will inevitably change,
and circumstances that get rearranged all too easily.

Remember that there's more to appreciate in this moment
than we realize. Believe me: Years from now, the truth of
this will shine. And one of your sincere regrets will be
not knowing how good you had it... at the time.

— Douglas Pagels

The Gift of Faith Having a Place in Your Life

As a knot appears unexpectedly in a thread, so disappointment blocks the smoothness of life. If a few deft strokes can untangle the skein, life continues evenly. But if it cannot be corrected, then it must be quietly woven into the design. Thus, the finished piece can still be beautiful — even though not as perfect as planned.

— Anonymous

We sleep, but the loom of life never stops and the pattern which was weaving when the sun went down — is weaving when it comes up tomorrow.

— Henry Ward Beecher

The sunrise never failed us yet.

— Celia Thaxter

For any weaving that needs to be done, God sends the threads.

— Italian Proverb

The Gift of a Life Filled with Love

Won't you come into the garden?
I would like my roses to see you.

— Richard Brinsley Sheridan

Love is the source of life.

— Susan Polis Schutz

Someone has written that love makes people believe in
immortality, because there seems not to be room enough
in life for so great a tenderness.

— Robert Louis Stevenson

We are each of us angels with only one wing.
And we can only fly by embracing each other.

— Luciano De Creschenzo

The Gift of a Real Friend

A friend is one of the nicest things you can have, and one of the best things you can be. A friend is a living treasure, and if you have one, you have one of the most valuable gifts in life.

A friend is the one who will always be beside you, through all the laughter, and through each and every tear. A friend is the one thing you can always rely on; the someone you can always open up to; the one wonderful person who always believes in you in a way that no one else seems to. A friend is a sanctuary. A friend is a smile.

A friend is a hand that is always holding yours, no matter where you are, no matter how close or far apart you may be. A friend is someone who is always there and will always — always — care. A friend is a feeling of forever in the heart.

A friend is the one door that is always open. A friend is the one to whom you can give your key. A friend is one of the nicest things you can have, and one of the best things you can be.

— Douglas Pagels

The Gift of Hanging In There and Holding On

The difficult we do immediately.
The impossible takes a little longer.

— Charles Alexandre de Calonne

When you must, you can.

— Jewish Proverb

You don't have to know how to sing.
It's feeling as though you want to
that makes the day worthwhile.

— Coleman Cox

Those who wish to sing always find a song.

— Swedish Proverb

The Gift of Being the Best You Can Be

Sometimes you
think that you
need to be perfect
that you cannot
make mistakes
At these times
you put so much
pressure on yourself
I wish you
would realize
that you are
a human being —
like everyone else
capable of
reaching great potential
but not capable of
being perfect

So please
just do your best
and realize that
this is enough
Don't compare yourself
to anyone
Be happy to be
the wonderful
unique, very special
person that you are

— Susan Polis Schutz

The Gift of a Child's Smile

Every... child on this earth has an overwhelming
desire to be loved, to be wanted, to be appreciated.
To the extent that we can fulfill this desire... will
we find happiness ourselves.

— Anonymous

Let the children be happy. Teach them to fill their hearts
with feelings of wonder and to be full of courage and
hope. Nothing is more important than the sharing of this
moment in time. Hold their kite strings, make their hearts
sing, make their smiles shine.

Reflect their inner and outer beauty. Encourage them to
be in less of a hurry. Love them each fleeting second. Try
to have the patience of a saint, and the understanding of
one, too. Admire them. Inspire them. And tell them in
untold ways what they mean to you.

— Douglas Pagels

The Gift of Lighting
Candles in the Lives of Others

If one life shines, the life next to it will catch the light.

— Anonymous

Go out of your way to be good to an older person. You can make somebody's entire day with a smile, a phone call, some flowers, or whatever it is you've got. Our elders have so much to give to those who listen, but they are the ones who deserve to receive. Don't pass up the chance to brighten their lives. An old adage reminds us that they need only a little, but they need that little — a lot.

— Douglas Pagels

It was only a glad "good morning"
As she passed along the way,
But it spread the morning's glory
Over the livelong day.

— Anonymous

The Gift of Keeping Life's Ups and Downs in Perspective

I've had my trials and troubles. The Lord has given me both vinegar and honey, but He has given me the vinegar with a teaspoon and the honey with a ladle.

— Attributed to William Bray

If you want to live more, you must master the art of appreciating the little, everyday blessings of life. This is not altogether a golden world, but there are countless gleams of gold to be discovered in it.

— Henry Alford Porter

If you haven't all the things you want, be grateful for the things you don't have that you didn't want.

— Anonymous

The Gift of Real Accomplishment

If we want to know what happiness is, we must seek it, not as if it were a pot of gold at the end of the rainbow, but among human beings who are living richly and fully the good life. If you observe a really happy man, you will find him building a boat, writing a symphony, educating his children, growing double dahlias in his garden. He will not be searching for happiness... he will have become aware that he is happy in the course of living twenty-four crowded hours in the day.

— W. Beran Wolfe

Sometimes it's important to work for that pot of gold. But other times it's essential to take time off and to make sure that your most important decision in the day simply consists of choosing which color to slide down on the rainbow.

— Douglas Pagels

The Gift of Finding Out
How Much Fun It Can Be

Cheerfulness keeps up a kind of delight in the mind, and fills it with a steady and perpetual serenity.

— Joseph Addison

Angels fly because they take themselves lightly.

— G. K. Chesterton

There aren't many things as therapeutic as smiles and laughter. Whenever you look at things in a lighter vein, it shows that your heart is in the right place.

— Douglas Pagels

Every survival kit should include a sense of humor.

— Anonymous

The Gift of Understanding
What Makes You So Outstanding

People go abroad to wonder at the height of mountains, at the huge waves of the sea, at the long courses of the rivers, at the vast compasses of the ocean... and they pass by themselves without even imagining.

— Augustine of Hippo

What the world is for us depends on what we are ourselves.

— Lewis G. Janes

Every individual is a marvel of unknown and unrealized possibilities.

— W. G. Jordon

You're an original, an individual, a masterpiece. Celebrate that; don't let your uniqueness make you shy. Don't be someone other than the wonder you are. Every star is important to the sky.

— Douglas Pagels

The Gift of Comprehending
What Others Are Going Through

Be kind. Everyone you meet is fighting a hard battle.

— John Watson

Go beyond yourself and reach out to other
people with a sincere love, respect, caring,
and understanding of their needs.

— Susan Polis Schutz

Resolve to be: tender with the young, compassionate
with the aged, sympathetic with the striving, and
tolerant of the weak and the wrong. There will be
times in your life when you will have been all of these.

— Anonymous

The Gift of Knowing How to Go with the Flow

Here is some gentle wisdom that will get you through just about anything: Appreciate, with all your heart, the best of life; do everything within your power to pass the tests of life; and learn how to live with the rest of life.

— Douglas Pagels

The deepest rivers flow with the least noise.

— Curt

Cooperation is doing with a smile what you have to do anyway.

— Anonymous

Things turn out best for the people who make the best of the way things turn out.

— Anonymous

The Gift of Imagining the Possibilities

The principle business of life is to enjoy it.

— Samuel Butler

Many of us have road maps we envision for the course we think our lives should take. It's important to get headed in the right direction, but don't get so caught up in the concerns over your destination that you forget to delight in the scenery of each new day. Remember that some of the secret joys of living are not found by rushing from point A to point B, but by inventing some imaginary letters along the way.

— Douglas Pagels

The truth is that everything
is a miracle and a wonder.

— Rabbi Barukh

Out of every earth day, make a little bit of heaven.

— Ella Wheeler Wilcox

The Gift of Giving Yourself Something Grand to Look Back On

The time will come when winter will ask you what you were doing all summer.

— Henry Clay

Off in the distance, I see an old man sitting in a comfortable chair beside an open fireplace. No, this is not a picture of my father or grandfather facing life's sunset — it is myself.

I have decided now, in my days of prime, to be kind to that old man.... It is said that old folks live in the past. I have resolved to give the old man some pleasant memories, some pleasant scenes to gaze upon. I want him to be able to look back and see deeds of kindness done, cheer brought into lonely hearts. I want him to look back upon some outstanding achievement.

I want to give the old man a quiet confidence in the future.

— Anonymous

The Gift of Going Beyond the Ordinary and Achieving Extraordinary Results

Don't be afraid to go out on a limb.
That's where the fruit is.

— Anonymous

Behold the turtle; he makes progress
only when he sticks his neck out.

— James Bryant Conant

It is not because things are difficult that we do not dare;
it is because we do not dare that they are difficult.

— Seneca

If you do what you've always done,
you'll get what you've always gotten.

— Anonymous

The Gift of Being Patient
with the Problems of Life

You must try to get along the best you can.

— Walt Whitman

When I want to consider a particular problem, I open a certain drawer. When I have settled the matter in my mind, I close that drawer and open another. When I desire to sleep, I close all the drawers.

— Napoleon

Have courage for the great sorrows of life and patience for the small ones; and when you have laboriously accomplished your daily task, go to sleep in peace. God is awake.

— Victor Hugo

The Gift of Knowing
that Everything Will Be Okay

Have patience. Everything is difficult before it is easy.

— Saadi

Nothing in life is to be feared. It is only to be understood.

— Marie Curie

If the sun and moon should doubt,
They'd immediately go out.

— William Blake

He who has a why to live for can bear almost any how.

— Friedrich Nietzsche

You have a future that is in the best of hands. Plan accordingly.

— Douglas Pagels

The Gift of Knowing that Beautiful Tomorrows Begin Today

Tomorrow is a beautiful road that will take you right where you want to go...

If you spend today walking away from worry and moving toward serenity; leaving behind conflict and traveling toward solutions; and parting with emptiness and never giving up on your search for fulfillment.
If you can do what works for you, your present will be happier and your path will be smoother. And best of all?

You'll be taking a step into a beautiful future.

— Douglas Pagels

The journey of a thousand miles begins with one step.

— Lao-Tzu

The Gift of Some of the Most Wonderful Wisdom of All

It is never too late
to be what you
might have been.

— George Eliot

We can bring so many blessings into our lives just by realizing that it is never too late. Before you turn the page on this day, make a pact with yourself to untie the ribbons and open the gifts we are given in this life. Do ordinary things in extraordinary ways. Have health and hope and happiness! Live a full life on this earth, understand your real worth, and wish on all your stars.

And don't ever forget, for even a day, how very special you are.

— Douglas Pagels

The Gift of Many Happy Returns

New journeys await you. Decisions lie ahead,
wondering what you will do, where you will go,
how you will choose when the choices are yours.

Remember that good decisions come back to bless
you, over and over again. Work for the ability
to choose wisely, to prosper, to succeed. Listen with
your heart as well as your head, to the glimmers
of truth that provide advice and inspiration to
the hours of your days. And let those truths take
you to beautiful places.

Touch the sky, and in your reach,
believe, achieve, and aspire.

I hope your tomorrows take you to the summit
of your goals, and your joys take you even higher.

— Douglas Pagels